World of Islam

Islam in Europe

MASON CREST PUBLISHERS
PHILADELPHIA

World of Islam

World of Islam

Islam in Europe

MICHAEL RADU

Editorial Consultants: Foreign Policy Research Institute, Philadelphia, PA

Mason Crest Publishers
370 Reed Road
Broomall, PA 19008
www.masoncrest.com

First printing

1 3 5 7 9 8 6 4 2

Library of Congress Cataloging-in-Publication Data

Radu, Michael.
  Islam in Europe / Michael Radu.
     p. cm. — (World of Islam)
  ISBN 978-1-4222-1363-6 (hardcover) — ISBN 978-1-4222-1366-7 (pbk.)
  1. Islam—Europe. 2. Muslims—Europe. I. Title.
  BP65.A1R33 2006
  305.6'97094—dc22
                            2009022080

Photo Credits: 7: Simon Cousins; 9: © OTTN Publishing; 11: Mark Kobayashi-Hilary; 12: Used under
license from Shutterstock, Inc.; 14: James Gordon; 17: Mark Kobayashi-Hilary; 19: JZ (http://commons.wiki
media.org/wiki/File:2007-05-07_rue_de_la_Roquette_Paris_P1010808.JPG), (inset) Mikael Marguerie; 21: Used
under license from Shutterstock, Inc.; 22: Used under license from Shutterstock, Inc.; 24: U.S. Department of
Defense; 25: Francis Tyers; (inset) La goutte de pluie; 27: Used under license from Shutterstock, Inc.; 29: James
Gordon; 30: Gryffindor; 34 (left) Cooperniall (www.flickr.com/photos/church-poverty), (right) Soman;
36: James Gordon; 39: Simon Cousins; 40: Richie Diesterheft, (inset) desdetasmania (www.flickr.com/
photos/desdetasmania); 43: David Shankbone (http://shankbone.org); 47: Used under license from Shutterstock,
Inc.; 49: Used under license from Shutterstock, Inc.; 52: Simon Cousins

Michael Radu, Ph.D., was a Senior Fellow at the Foreign Policy Research Institute (FPRI) in Philadelphia and Co-chair of
FPRI's Center on Terrorism, Counter-terrorism and Homeland Security. He was the author or editor of many books, including
Europe's Ghost: Islamism and Jihad in Western Europe (2009), *Dilemmas of Democracy and Dictatorship: Place, Time and
Ideology* (2006), *Islamist and Terrorist Groups in Asia* (2005), and *Dangerous Neighborhood: Contemporary Issues in Turkey's
Foreign Policy* (2002). Dr. Radu died in March 2009.

World of Islam

Table of Contents

Introduction

*I*ssues related to Islam and Muslims in the United States or in the West in general only came to the attention of most Americans recently, after the terrorist attacks of September 11, 2001. Whether or not it's fair, since 9/11, most Americans' concerns with Islam are related to violence and terrorism.

Muslims in America are a relatively small minority, usually estimated at less than 3 percent of the total population. By comparison, many European countries have proportionally much larger Muslim communities. The number of Muslims in France is larger than that of Muslims in the United States, although France's total population is five times smaller.

Moreover, the nature of Muslims in the United States is distinct from those in Europe in terms of origins. While the number of converts to Islam in Europe is small—in the tens of thousands at most (although this number is growing)—almost half of American

Two young Muslims at a street-side prayer service, London. More than 1.6 million Muslims live in the United Kingdom.

Muslims are converts, and the converts are overwhelmingly African American. Therefore, in most respects Muslims in the United States are ethnically, socially, and demographically distinct from those in Europe.

It is difficult to determine the total number of Muslims in Europe with any accuracy because many are illegal immigrants, and thus are hard to count. (Europe is herein defined as the 15 member states of the European Union prior to EU's expansion after 2004: France, Germany, Italy, the Netherlands, Belgium, Luxembourg, the United Kingdom, Spain, Portugal, Sweden, Denmark, Ireland, Greece, Finland, and Austria. These countries are often known collectively as Western Europe.) Moreover, countries like France, which among European nations has the largest number of Muslims, prohibit by law the inclusion of religion in census data. Furthermore, even legal immigrants often have not become citizens and thus are missed by censuses. The best assessment today is that there are some 20 million people of Muslim background in Western Europe. Some recent reliable figures, from 2005, are listed in the chart on the opposite page.

However, as an example of how unreliable these figures are, the Moroccan government, whose figures would presumably be more accurate because that country is more interested in this matter, claims that there are 1.6 million Moroccan citizens in France and 700,000 in Spain. That does not include the hundreds of thousands of Moroccans in the Netherlands, Belgium, and Italy. And at least in France, the largest number of Muslims are not Moroccans but Algerians.

Numbers and Origins

It is important to look at absolute numbers, as well as the proportion of Muslims to the general population, because these numbers help explain the official and popular reactions to immi-

Europe's Muslim Communities, 1990–2005

Country	1990			2005		
	Muslim Population	% of Total Population	Countries of Origin	Muslim Population	% of Total Population	Growth
Belgium	335,000	3.4%	Morocco, Turkey	371,000	3.6%	+36,000
Denmark	55,000	1%	Morocco, Somalia, Turkey	114,000	2.1%	+59,000
France	4 Million	7%	Algeria, Morocco	5 Million	8.2%	+1 Million
Germany	2.9 Million	3.6%	Turkey	3.7 Million	4.5%	+800,000
Italy	600,000	1.1%	Morocco, Albania	1 Million	1.8%	+400,000
The Netherlands	533,000	3.6%	Turkey, Morocco	804,000	4.9%	+271,000
Spain	170,000	0.5%	Morocco	427,000	1%	+257,000
Sweden	137,000	1.6%	Turkey, Southeast Asia	179,000	2%	+42,000
UK	1.05 Million	1.9%	Africa, Southeast Asia, Middle East	1.64 Million	2.2%	+590,000

Source: Europe's Muslim Communities, *Wall Street Journal* online.

grants. If the number of Muslim immigrants is small, the local or national reaction should be expected to be limited or positive; if the numbers are large and, most importantly recent, then one can expect the national reaction to be sharply different, and it is.

This phenomenon must be understood in light of European countries' historical origins as slowly developed, ethnically homogeneous entities. France, Germany, and England, for example, all defined their identity for centuries according to their inhabitants' common language, religion, and history. All of that is challenged by the rapidly growing numbers of recently arrived immigrants from areas of different religion, ethnicity, and traditions. In fact, the majority of European states not only are nation-states, but also have historically been countries of emigration, rather than immigration. The United States, by contrast, has long been a destination for migrants.

Muslim immigrants to Europe bring with them some of the customs and traditions of their home countries—just as, for example, Mexican immigrants to the United States bring part of their culture with them. This means that today's immigrants from mostly secular states such as Turkey are more likely to accept the separation of religion and state found in countries like Germany or the Netherlands than are Palestinians or Pakistanis who immigrate to the United Kingdom.

The larger the number of immigrants to a certain country or area, the more likely it is that the immigrants will maintain the customs, traditions, and habits of their countries of origin. Hence a visitor to certain parts of Berlin or the northeastern London metropolitan area could easily get by speaking Turkish, Kurdish, or Urdu and eating Middle Eastern food, never feeling that he or she is in Germany or England.

In some cases—especially that of recent refugees, such as Somalis or Sudanese, who are accepted in Europe more than in any other place—customs like female genital mutilation, polygamy (multiple wives), and "honor killings" (the murder of women by family members for their relationships or marriages with partners who are rejected by the family) are common even though they are illegal under the laws of the accepting state. This produces both social and political problems.

As in the case of immigrants to Germany or the Netherlands from Turkey, ethnicity is more important than religion or original

South Asians make up more than 3 percent of the United Kingdom's total population (Indians, 1.8 percent; Pakistanis, 1.3 percent), according to the 2001 UK census. This photo is from London.

citizenship in explaining how immigrants will conduct themselves. For instance, many Kurds—who are legally considered Turks in most of Europe, whether they are from Turkey, Iran, or Syria—are neither Shia nor Sunni but Alevis (a sect of Islam widely supported in Turkey and parts of Syria). They are also likely to be supporters of separatist organizations fighting against the Turkish government.

Muslim immigrants to Europe do not necessarily become separated from developments in their countries of origin. In fact, many Muslims in Europe, especially youth, are attracted by radical Islam's ideology, including calls to violence. They are therefore perceived as a threat by the majority population among which they live—as demonstrated in England, Germany, and France, countries that have strengthened anti-terrorist legislation since 9/11. And indeed, attempts by radical Islamist groups, individuals, or cells to engage in terrorist attacks against the Western countries in which they live (including the United States) are numerous. Most of these groups or cells are linked to foreign countries such as Pakistan or Palestinian areas in the Middle East.

Country Profiles

Belgium. Muslims in Belgium are mostly of Moroccan and Turkish (or Kurdish) origin and are concentrated around Brussels, where they tend to self-segregate from Arab or sub-Saharan Muslim immigrants. Those living in majority Flemish areas such as Antwerp are under increasing pressure from Flemish nationalists seeking immigration controls.

A view of Brussels. Most of Belgium's Muslims—who are primarily of Moroccan, Turkish, or Kurdish extraction—live in or around the capital city.

France. By all assessments, France has the largest Muslim community in the West. The most recent French figures, approximate as they are, indicate that 5 million to 6 million Muslims live in France, out of a total population of about 62 million. Of the Muslims in France, an estimated 1.5 million are of Algerian origin, 1 million are Moroccan, 400,000 are Tunisian, 340,000 are sub-Saharan Africans (mostly from Mali and Senegal), and 320,000 are Turkish. The rest have various other, mostly Middle Eastern origins. The number of practicing Muslims, defined as those who frequently visit a mosque, is estimated at 20 percent of the total. Only a third of Muslims in France think that a Muslim believer should follow the precepts of the Qur'an—the holy book of Islam—even when they conflict with French law, and some 80 percent consider secularism positively. Between 2 million and 3 million Muslims are French citizens.

Germany. Most of Germany's nearly 2 million Muslims are of "Turkish" origin (the quotation marks are necessary because, although originally from Turkey, almost half of those are ethnically Kurdish rather than Turkish, an important distinction). Indeed, Kurds in Germany speak an Iranian language unrelated to Turkish, are generally hostile to the Turkish government and Turks in general, and disproportionately support autonomy, if not independence, for the Kurdish-majority areas of Turkey.

Spain. Muslims in Spain are a peculiar group and have proven the most difficult for a European country to integrate. For centuries the Iberian Peninsula (most of today's Spain and Portugal) was under Muslim control. And most of the recent immigrants come from Morocco, the same area from which the Moors launched their conquest of Iberia in 711. The Spanish *Reconquista*, or reconquest, was completed in 1492. But Islamic thought calls for the recovery of all Muslim lands lost to Christians. Many Muslims in Spain, especially converts to Islam, advocate the return of historically important Moorish sites to Muslim use. These sites include, for example, the Grand Mosque of Córdoba, which was later converted into a Catholic cathedral. Not surprisingly, such views do not foster assimilation of Muslims.

The Netherlands. The Muslim population of the Netherlands is mostly divided between Moroccans and Turks (including Kurds from Turkey); some 20 percent are immigrants from other Muslim areas in North Africa and elsewhere. While Turks in Amsterdam tend to keep to themselves and remain aloof from

An interior view of the Mezquita de Córdoba, or Grand Mosque of Córdoba. Begun in 784, the mosque was completed about two centuries later. It was converted into a Catholic cathedral after King Ferdinand III of Castile captured Córdoba from the Moors in 1236.

the Dutch environment, the Moroccans, especially the young, often choose to challenge the existing laws and social rules.

United Kingdom. The more than 2 million Muslims in the United Kingdom—almost all of them living in England—are predominantly from the Indian Subcontinent, or former British India (now Pakistan, India, and Bangladesh). Many, if not most, of the largest group (Pakistanis) come from the Kashmir area, which is still hotly disputed between Pakistan and India. Most of the Bangladeshis come from the rural area of Sylhet. This is important because it explains the challenges both groups face in assimilating into British society. Kashmiris are radicalized and often susceptible to Islamic fundamentalist preachers; Bangladeshis in Britain face the double challenge of adapting to a mostly urban environment as well as a culturally alien one. Both groups are inherently hostile to the large Hindu and Sikh communities in Britain; these attitudes originated in the postwar partition of British India in 1947.

In other West European countries, the growing Muslim presence has led to a sharp reaction. For example, Switzerland—where Muslims now make up about 4.3 percent of the population (they are mostly of Bosnian and Albanian origin)—has seen a rise in anti-immigration and anti-Muslim political parties.

The Muslim Immigrant Experience in Europe

Because of the expansion of the Ottoman Empire, significant Muslim communities have existed in the Balkan Peninsula region (including the European part of Turkey, Bulgaria, Bosnia and Herzegovina, Serbia, Kosovo, and Albania) since the 14th century. The presence of large numbers of Muslims in Western Europe, however, is a recent phenomenon, dating mostly from the 1960s. The post–World War II economic growth of that region led to an acute shortage of labor. France, Germany, and the Netherlands invited guest workers from Turkey and North Africa (Morocco, Algeria, and Tunisia) to fill the gap. Meanwhile, for similar reasons and following decolonization, large numbers of immigrants from the former British India immigrated to Britain in search of work.

Who Are Europe's Muslim Immigrants?

Today, as seen in the table on page 9, the majority of Muslims in Europe come from the few countries and areas that provided the bulk of emigrants during the 1960s—Turkey in the case of Germany, North Africa (Algeria and Morocco) in the case of France, and the Indian Subcontinent in the case of Great Britain.

In addition, during the 1990s large numbers of Bosnian and Albanian Muslims emigrated from Yugoslavia as that country was torn apart by civil war. Many of these people went to Switzerland. The Netherlands and the Scandinavian countries of Sweden and

In recent decades, most of the Muslims who have immigrated to Europe have done so for economic reasons. But because many have low levels of education and do not possess advanced job skills, they often face poverty in their adopted countries.

Denmark have received millions of sub-Saharan Africans (from Senegal, Mali, and Mauritania) as well as many Somalis fleeing their collapsing nation since 1991. More recently, many Iraqis and Iranians (as well as Lebanese Christians) have moved to countries such as Sweden.

European countries have accepted proportionally more refugees and asylum seekers than the United States (albeit fewer in absolute terms). During the past two decades, however, the majority of Muslims moving to Europe have been neither refugees nor asylum seekers, but economic migrants and their families. This is an important point to consider, since the overwhelming majority of economic migrants everywhere, Muslim or otherwise, tend to come from low-education, low-skill backgrounds. They also tend to have larger families. During the 1960s, European countries such as France, Germany, and the United Kingdom especially needed workers in low-skill sectors such as construction. The first generation of Muslim economic migrants fit the bill, and the great need for their labor ensured decent wages. Today, however, European countries have service-oriented economies, in which high skills are at a premium. Developing countries' immigrants are, by necessity, filling poorly paid positions. Thus, the standard of living for these immigrants remains near the bottom in their adopted homes.

Barriers to Integration

Most of the 2 million Arab-Americans living in the United States—about 60 percent—are Christians. The Arab-American community also ranks above the national average in education and income. This is not at all true of Europe. There, most Arabs are Muslims, and many are poorly educated, unemployed, and living in the crime-infested suburbs of large cities.

In the suburbs of cities such as Paris, London, and Amsterdam, thousands of immigrant youths, most of them Muslim, live hopeless lives and react in anarchic ways. The 2007 riots in the suburbs of Paris, in which most of those involved were Muslims, are but one example.

Throughout Europe, the influence of outside radical organizations constitutes a growing security threat. Pakistan-based radical organizations, for example, include groups linked to al-Qaeda. North Africa has its own al-Qaeda-associated group, al-Qaeda in Islamic Maghreb.

An increasingly serious social, cultural, and security problem is the evolution of second-generation, Europe-born Muslims

The May 2007 election of Nicolas Sarkozy as France's president triggered these scenes of unrest in the streets of Paris. Sarkozy had earlier offended French Muslims with comments they perceived as condescending and even Islamophobic—including his observation that Muslims in France should be obligated to respect the country's laws, to refrain from oppressing girls or taking more than one wife, and to stop slaughtering sheep at their homes.

who do not see integration and assimilation into their countries as desirable but who instead retreat into the notion of the global Islamic community, the *umma*. Many of these people are young. Their choice—a rejection of integration and common values—may provoke strong responses from majority groups. Such responses include calls for anti-immigration (and sometimes anti-Islamic) legislation, which in turn leads to claims of racism, discrimination, and repression.

One has to be wary of the claims of both sides in the European Islam debate. Many Muslim organizations claim that any criticism of any Muslim practice—whether polygamy, honor killings, or forced marriages (a common occurrence among Pakistani, Turkish, and Somali immigrants)—constitutes "Islamophobia" (hatred of Islam) or "racism." On the other hand, growing populism and nationalism in some European countries (especially Denmark, the Netherlands, and Austria) tends to falsely associate all immigrants with Muslims and Islam and all Muslims with terrorism and practices unacceptable or illegal in Europe. These are all demagogic, unfair, and intolerant claims.

Whatever one may think about Islam, the fact remains that Muslims are in Europe and will remain in Europe, and their numbers are likely to grow. The issue of Islam in European countries cannot be ignored. Native Europeans will have to live with the reality of millions of Muslims living in their midst. For their part, European Muslims may have to accept some degree of integration or even assimilation.

Statistics from the German Federal Office of Labor showed that 25 percent of Turks in Germany were jobless in 2003, compared with just over 10 percent of native-born Germans. In Turkish areas of Berlin, unemployment in 2005 was 52 percent, compared with a German national average of about 12 percent.

It should be pointed out that those figures were from a period of relative economic growth in Germany. Similar data from every European country indicate that Muslims are one of the most economically disadvantaged groups. Why is that so?

To begin with, most Muslims in Europe are either immigrants or second-generation descendants of immigrants. That means that, like all immigrants, they start with clear disadvantages, such as language and education. Moreover, many Muslim immigrants are from some of most backward areas in their countries of origin: Eastern Anatolia in the case of the Kurds, the Rif Mountains for Moroccans, Kashmir for Pakistanis, and so on. That means they have to make the transition not only between countries and cultural environments but also between rural and

A village in Kashmir. Muslims who migrate from the Kashmir region—like Muslim migrants from other underdeveloped or rural areas—often find it difficult to adjust to life in urban Europe.

overwhelmingly urban societies. Indeed, it is one thing for a relatively cosmopolitan Moroccan from Casablanca to move to Amsterdam, and another for a Berber-speaking person from the Rif to do so.

Then there are the social customs of most rural peoples—and that means most Muslim immigrants to Europe—whereby women are not only seen as inferior, but also as responsible for child-rearing and nothing more. Given the typically large number of children in Muslim families in Europe, this means that the vast majority of wives cannot enter the labor market, thereby limiting the family's income. Moreover, by staying home, as most do, Muslim women limit their knowledge of European culture and habits—for both themselves and their young children. It is common to find Turkish immigrant women in Germany who do not speak German after decades of living in Berlin.

The burqa—a garment that covers almost all of a woman's body—is a common sight in places like Pakistan and Afghanistan, where Islam's injunction to dress modestly is interpreted strictly. But, as this photo shows, burqa-wearing women can also be seen on the streets of Europe's cities—a visible symbol of some Muslims' resistance to assimilation into European society.

The lack of integration for many, poor academic performance, and, recently, Europe's economic stagnation have all combined to produce large numbers of young Muslims with few hopes, high rates of criminality (up to 60 percent of inmates in some French prisons are Muslim), and an identity crisis. Indeed, for young Muslims born in Europe, the cultural and even linguistic ties with the countries their parents came from have been lost, without the young Muslims in Europe becoming, or being accepted as, French, English, or German. It is not surprising, then, that for growing numbers of such Muslims, religion becomes the default identity, and many are attracted by radical interpretations of Islam, some of which lead to violence and terrorism, or that many are recruited by radical Islamists while in jail.

Finally, there is a clear disparity between Muslim women and men in Europe in educational terms, with the former much more likely to be better educated and integrated, at least among the second generation. The result, paradoxically, is that many men choose uneducated but submissive spouses from the rural areas of their countries of origin rather than European Muslim ones. This continues the cycle of resistance to integration, which in turn perpetuates an inferior economic status and more political grievances.

European Resistance to Muslim Immigration

Because European countries have long defined themselves as nations—homogeneous in terms of ethnicity, customs, and language—absorbing a large number of culturally and religiously alien immigrants has raised many political and social problems. In addition, since most immigrants to Europe are now illegal, the world economic recession that began in 2008 has put additional pressure on governments to control the influx.

Of course, the way European Muslim immigrants behave and are received in their new country depends to a large degree on the

Among a small segment of second-generation European Muslims, radical Islam—and even Osama bin Laden's calls for jihad against the West—holds appeal.

immigrants' country of origin, and the strength of their ties to that country. Thus, the Turks, who are mostly present in Germany and the Netherlands and who come from a largely secular society, are less interested in radical Islamist activities. Moreover, their different language and customs set them apart from other Muslim immigrant communities. On the one hand, Pakistanis (and to a lesser extent Bangladeshi and Indian Muslims) in England and, increasingly, in the Catalonia region of Spain come from and keep close ties with their home country, the world's most radicalized Islamic country. As a consequence they are often deemed to represent a major security threat—an assessment reinforced by the terrorist attacks in London in July 2005.

On the other hand, Muslim Pakistanis and sub-Saharan immigrants, especially Malians and Somalis, bring to Europe unpopular cultural customs that are unrelated to, but often mistakenly associated with, Islam. These customs, including female

(Above) Ambulances and emergency personnel at the ready in London's Russell Square, near the site of a suicide bombing on a subway train, July 7, 2005. During morning rush hour that day, four British Muslims attacked London's transit system, killing 52 people and injuring more than 700. (Inset) A subway passenger trapped underground after one of the bombings took this photo with his cell phone.

genital mutilation and "honor killings," give some Europeans the impression that Muslims in general are incompatible with local values and laws.

Furthermore, European judiciary traditions, as well as immigration laws that were formerly quite liberal, allowed radical, even terrorist, organizations that were defeated or persecuted in Muslim-majority countries such as Algeria, Morocco, and Pakistan to establish recruitment, fund-raising, and ideological bases in Europe. This is especially true in England.

Muslim Organizations in Europe

Europe's millions of Muslims have religious, cultural, and ethnic backgrounds that are as diverse as the countries from which they originated. In addition, the diversity of beliefs among Muslims is no different from the diversity of beliefs among Christians, who could be Catholics, Protestants, Evangelicals, or Eastern Orthodox, among other denominations. Thus, one must look at Muslims in Europe as they really are—a culturally, ethnically, and confessionally diverse community whose only common link is their acceptance of the Qur'an as revealed truth. But they interpret its contents in diverse, culturally specific manners.

For instance, the main division of Islam—between the Sunnis (who make up about 85 percent of Muslims worldwide), Shias (who make up about 14 percent), and other tiny groups (Deobandis, Barelvis)—is represented in Europe as well. But the

A copy of the Qur'an, Islam's sacred scriptures. Muslims believe the Qur'an records the actual words of God, as dictated in Arabic to the Prophet Muhammad by an angel. Still, they interpret the contents of the Qur'an in culturally specific ways.

Shias, almost all of whom are Iranians or are subsidized by Tehran, constitute just 2 or 3 percent of the Muslims in Europe.

The Sunnis in Europe are diverse as well. The two major divisions are between moderates, often supported by the governments of their countries of origin (Morocco, Algeria, Pakistan, Turkey), and radicals, or Salafis, supported by Saudi Arabia and other Persian Gulf countries. Some of the radicals support or belong to Islamist terrorist organizations or to various Pakistani fundamentalist and violent organizations.

In many European countries, Muslim organizations are either ethnically based (for example, Turkish, Pakistani, Algerian, or Moroccan, to mention just the four largest groups) or pan-Islamic (general, cross-ethnic, and cross-language, based solely on the common religion). Of the pan-Islamic groups, the Muslim Brotherhood is the most active, wealthiest (from Saudi money) pan-Islamic organization in Europe. Founded in Egypt in 1928, it seeks the unification of a pure Islam everywhere—by violence in some places (Gaza), by missionary work elsewhere (Europe, the United States, Jordan). The Tabligh ("The Conveying Group") has similar goals to the Muslim Brotherhood, but it seeks a global Muslim state—a caliphate—as its ultimate goal. Both groups, and others like them, actively oppose Muslim integration into the Christian or secular European societies.

Considering the extraordinary sectarian and ethnic diversity of the Muslim communities in Europe, one has to begin any analysis of Muslim/Islamic organizations with a major caveat regarding their representativeness. For instance, ethnic Turks and Turkish Kurdish immigrants in Germany or the Netherlands are not alike in their views of and commitment to Islam. Nor are they equally influenced by Ankara. Ethnic Turks still receive their imams from among those vetted by Turkey's secular government, whereas Turkish Kurds are more influenced by the secular, indeed Marxist Kurdish, secessionist organization PKK (Kurdistan Workers' Party).

As for the Muslims in Britain, whether through language (Urdu, Bengali, Pushtu) or their interpretation of Islam (more fundamentalist Deobandis, moderate Barelvis), they are even more diverse. In France, at least one estimate considers that as many as 40 percent of Muslims are non-practicing (at least beyond some traditional customs). Berbers and Arabs are not friendly to each other there. For all these reasons, the institutional place of Islam in Europe is still in some flux.

These cleavages strongly suggest that Islam in Europe is quite different from the other religions, inasmuch as it is not only

A member of the Kurdistan Workers' Party (known in English by the acronym PKK). Since the 1980s, the PKK has been waging a violent campaign against Turkey to create an independent Kurdish state.

divided along doctrinal and ethnic lines, but—especially among the majority Sunnis—lacks a real clergy and hierarchy. Accordingly, when various governments sought to establish a legal relationship between the state and Islam, they found it very difficult to do so in the absence of countrywide representative Muslim bodies. Either those bodies had to be established by the governments themselves, or the states had to deal with organizations controlled from abroad, by various governments of Islamic states.

In most European countries, governments have tried—and usually failed—to treat Muslim communities as yet another distinct religious group. The French Council of Muslim Religion (CFCM) is a case in point. Established by the French government, it was always divided among Algerian or Moroccan-controlled or pan-Islamic organizations such as the Muslim Brotherhood. The reason was almost always the reality of

Islam's divisions—ethnic and theological—and the competing influences of the countries of origin.

Add to all of this the inherently weak institutional tradition of Sunni Islam and its own divisions among four legal schools, and any government attempt to establish, recognize, or help a "national" Muslim organization seems to be doomed. None of that means, however, that large Muslim organizations, some transcending national and ethnic boundaries, do not exist or that some do not have significant followings.

The situation in the five largest European countries, which are also those with the largest and most diverse Muslim populations, is important to understand.

France

Muslim associations have formed several federations to identify and represent common interests vis-à-vis the state. For the moment, those associations remain the principal medium for

The Mosquée de Paris (Paris Mosque).

communication between the state and Muslim communities. Several national organizations have sought recognition as the official state representative of the Muslim community. These include the National Federation of the Muslims of France (FNMF), which is controlled from and subsidized by Morocco; the Paris Mosque, controlled and subsidized by Algeria; and the Union of the Islamic Organizations of France (UOIF), a Muslim Brotherhood–controlled group, mostly subsidized from Saudi Arabia and other Gulf states. In addition, the Tabligh, a pan-Islamic, missionary organization financed by individuals and some governments from Gulf countries, has its European head-quarters in England but is banned in France (as well as most of continental Europe) since it is known to offer the indoctrination leading many Muslims to terrorism.

Germany

Three umbrella organizations exist on the national level in Germany. Each claims to represent all Muslims in the country, but in fact none does. These are not religious communities but political interest groups: (1) Islamrat für die Bundesrepublik Deutschland (Islamic Congress of Islam in the Federal Republic of Germany); (2) Zentralrat für die Muslime in Deutschland (Central Congress of Muslims in Germany); and (3) Diyanet, the Turkish directorate of religious affairs.

On the regional level, in Germany's states, coalitions of local Muslim communities have emerged. In contrast to the umbrella groups, these coalitions claim the status of religious communities and try to represent the majority of Islamic communities in the country. Why this is so depends on the legal situation. The German constitution stipulates that religion formally falls within the responsibility of the states, and the government has only an informal function of issuing directives.

Important religious coalitions exist in individual states like Hessen, Berlin, and Hamburg.

Italy

Italy is a good example of a government trying with little success to form an organized Muslim partner. The Christian denominations, through various concordats and agreements with the Italian state since 1929, have all established clear legal frameworks in their relations with Rome. Islam, however, has not. The reason is that Muslim organizations in Italy are so badly split and competing in their claims of being recognized that no government could ask Parliament to decide whom to talk to. Moreover, none is plausibly representative of all or even most Muslims in Italy. Equally important, the rivalries between Muslim organizations in Italy are exacerbated by the direct interference of foreign governments, especially Saudi Arabia and Morocco, which control "their" organizations and use their political influence on the Italian government to promote the legitimacy of their organizations. Thus the fragmentation and politicization of Islam in Italy—as in other countries such as France and Germany—has prevented the establishment of an adequate legal framework for the relationship between Islam and the state.

The Union of Islamic Community and Organizations in Italy (UCOII) claims to be the most representative Muslim organization in Italy. But its own polling suggests that the great majority of Muslims in Italy belong to no organization.

Other groups include the Islamic Association Zayd ibn Thabit and the Union of Italian Muslims. The latter has only a few members. However, this minor group has attracted the most disproportionate media and political attention in Italy during the past few years. It has sued, in part successfully, the Vatican and the Italian state over the presence of crucifixes in schools. The

Union of Italian Muslims also sued journalist Oriana Fallacci over supposed "insults to Islam" in one of her books.

Spain

The Islamic Council of Spain (CIE) is a key organization in that country. Commenting on the CIE's demand to share praying areas and time in the Córdoba Cathedral, spokeswoman Isabel Romero claimed that "we want to give our support to the universal character of this building" and that in no way "is this request about reclaiming our rights—far less any kind of reconquest." However, the group does not appear to see the Damascus Grand Mosque or Hagia Sofia in Istanbul as having a similar "universal character."

A similar type of attitude is represented by Abdennur Prado, secretary of the Junta Islámica en España (the Islamic Board in Spain), for whom "The problem of Islamophobia is an urgent reality in countries like the United States, France, Germany, Netherlands, Belgium or Spain. In all of these one has lived through attacks against Muslims for the simple fact of being such as representatives of this 'other' who is not accepted on one's 'own' territory. The fascist tide grows under the shelter of institutions, too preoccupied to fight against a hypothetical Islamist fundamentalism to realize that the most urgent problem of the West is Islamophobia."

The United Kingdom

The main Islamic organization in the United Kingdom is the Muslim Council of Britain (MCB). It describes itself as "an umbrella organization dedicated to the common good, to the betterment of the community and country." Formed in 1997 by representatives of more than 250 Muslim organizations from all parts of Britain, including Northern Ireland, the MCB considers

(Above) Muhammad Abdul Bari of the Muslim Council of Britain (MCB) speaks at a conference on the issue of poverty in Great Britain, December 6, 2006. (Inset) The flag of Jamaat-e-Islami, a Pakistan-based radical Islamist organization that critics say is closely linked to the MCB.

itself "a vibrant coalition of grassroots organizations and institutions and individual talent and skills that is making a positive and constructive contribution to meeting the needs and the aspirations of the Muslim community in a period of recurring crises and anxious optimism." All of these claims are challenged by many Muslims in Britain, especially young Muslims.

The mostly Arab Muslim Brotherhood (whose closest allies in the United Kingdom are the Muslim Association of Britain) and its South Asian counterpart in Pakistan, Jamaat-e-Islami (whose supporters control the MCB), share the same pan-Islamic ideology. Some of their branches are engaged in violence. Nevertheless, many among the British establishment reason that these groups are not part of al-Qaeda, which is true; that they are growing in power, which is regrettably true as well; and that they are composed of reasonable men with whom Britain can do business, which is patently untrue.

Demographic Trends and Security Threats

Although all generalizations about immigrants attract accusations of racism, scientific studies do offer an image of the sociological origins and characteristics of immigrants to Europe, Muslim or not, and those are useful to examine. To begin with, immigrants tend to come from the same regions of their countries of origin. For example, most Italian-Americans came from southern Italy and Sicily. In the case of Muslims in England, many came from the disputed area of Kashmir, which was partitioned between India and Pakistan after World War II. Bangladeshis in England tend to have come from in and around Sylhet. France's Muslims came mostly from specific regions of Algeria, such as Kabylia. Spain's Muslims came largely from northern Morocco (Tangiers and Tétouan). Most ethnic Turks in Germany, France, and the Netherlands came from central Anatolia, and the Turkish Kurds from southeastern Anatolia.

Virtually all Muslim immigrants to Europe came from rural areas, have low levels of education and skills, and are socially and religiously conservative.

Second-generation Muslims in Europe—who constitute a majority by now—are, generally speaking, less integrated, earn less, and have lower standards of living than the majority population around them. Many feel that they are somehow placed between natives and immigrants, unable to belong to either group. Some seek total assimilation—half of the Muslims born

A Kurdish shepherd, northern Iraq. Most Muslim immigrants to Europe come from rural areas.

in France do not go to a mosque, for example—but many use their religion as a default position for rejecting the society around them. In fact, the latter attitude is a good explanation for the disproportionate presence of Muslims in the criminal population of Europe.

Growth in the Muslim Population

Some Europeans worry that the Muslim population's high demographic growth—through continuous immigration and large families—could in a few decades change the ethnic structure of their countries. This is especially true of smaller countries, such as Denmark, Belgium, and the Netherlands. Some of these fears are overblown. For example, the French-Muslim population (at least those legally born in France) has low rates of growth very similar to those of native French. Still, there is a trend—especially in the Netherlands and Germany—of local Muslim men marrying in their country of origin, and thus "importing" a tradition of large families, of mothers staying at home (and thus lower family income), and of resistance to cultural assimilation.

Thus the problem is not just the Muslim population's size but also the demographic trends. A 2005 Pew study of Muslims in Europe reported:

Muslims still only make up a small portion of Europe's population, no more than about 5 percent of the EU's more than 425 million people. But most demographers predict that that number will increase dramatically in the coming decades—to 10 percent as early as 2020. Indeed, if the past is any guide, that estimate may be low, since the size of the European Muslim community has tripled in the last 30 years.

This rapid growth is caused both by immigration and high Muslim birthrates. Nearly one million legal immigrants enter Europe each year, mostly on family reunification visas or as refugees seeking asylum. A majority of these newcomers are from North Africa, Turkey and other Islamic countries. Muslims also make up a large share of the continent's illegal immigrants—a group that is estimated to number up to half a million per year.

At the same time, Muslims already living on the continent are having three times as many children as their native European neighbors. This trend can be seen in the relative youth of European Muslims. In Germany, for instance, fully one-third of all Muslims are under 18, compared to less than one-fifth of the population as a whole. And in Great Britain and Belgium, one-third of all Muslims are under age 15, compared to one-fifth of the general populations of those countries. The fact that this sizable young cohort is approaching its peak child-producing years should help drive Muslim numbers up. "Given the age spread of the Muslim population, their numbers would grow quite a bit even if immigration stopped tomorrow," says Furman University Professor Brent Nelsen, an expert on religion in Europe. Meanwhile, low native birthrates throughout the continent will further increase the Muslim share of the entire population. Indeed, with a birthrate of 1.45 children per couple, the European Union is expected to shrink from 455 million today to 425 million in 2050, even if current immigration levels remain constant. Moreover, with Europe's aging population putting an increasing strain on the continent's generous health and pension schemes, much greater immigration may be necessary to maintain a workforce large enough to pay benefits to retirees.

Security Threats

Many Americans, remembering 9/11, believe that the Islamist threat is mostly directed at the United States. That is not correct. Europe has been the victim of more violent attacks from Muslim fundamentalists than has the United States, and the number of

The average age of European Muslims is considerably lower than the average age of the general population on the continent. With a larger proportion of Muslims in (or soon to enter) their childbearing years—and with the higher birthrates that exist among Muslims—demographers predict that the percentage of Europeans who are Muslims will rise significantly in the coming decades.

failed terrorist attacks and arrests in Europe far surpasses those in the United States. Moreover, in several European countries an attack by radical Islamists has produced a psychological impact similar to the impact that 9/11 had on Americans. These attacks include the March 11, 2004, bombings on Madrid's commuter-train system, which killed 191 people killed and wounded 1,755 others; the November 4, 2004, murder in Amsterdam of Dutch film director Theo van Gogh, who had offended Islamic fundamentalists with a film about the treatment of women in Islam; and the July 7, 2005, bombings on London's public transportation system, which killed 52 people and injured more than 700.

(Below) Red candles outside Madrid's Atocha Station commemorate the victims of the March 11, 2004, terrorist attacks. Islamist radicals detonated 10 bombs on four commuter trains, killing 191 people and injuring about 2,000. (Inset) A crane removes destroyed rail cars.

In addition, Islamist violence in Europe has a much longer history than in the United States. As early as 1994, bombs planted by Algeria's Armed Islamic Group (GIA) killed seven people in the Paris subway. On Christmas Eve of that year, the GIA tried, and failed, to use a hijacked plane to destroy the Eiffel Tower.

In almost all cases, the Muslim perpetrators of terrorist attacks in Europe had links to radical Islamist groups in their countries of origin. In other words, a number of Muslim immigrants—a minority, to be sure—brought to Europe the Islamist radicalism of their home countries, or their Europe-born children joined such groups, whether at home or by undergoing indoctrination and training in those countries (Pakistan, Algeria, Turkey).

Moreover, many European countries had very lax immigration laws and accepted radicals' claims of asylum. The United Kingdom, for example, became a true haven for Algerian fundamentalists rejected in France because of their past history of violence. Equally important, certain European countries—the United Kingdom once again most prominent among them—granted political asylum to individuals known to be close to al-Qaeda and to serve as ideologues, recruiters, and fund-raisers for that organization or groups close to it. Among those individuals were Abu Qatada, now under arrest in Britain, Abu Bakri (expelled to Lebanon), and Abu Hamza (awaiting extradition to the United States). The fact that citizens and residents of the European Union could travel freely from Finland to Portugal and from Ireland to Romania and Estonia allowed such individuals to spread their ideology and activities throughout the continent.

Acceptance of Muslims in Europe

In most European countries—especially as Muslim immigration in large numbers is of recent origin—the integration of Muslims is problematic. Some Muslim groups, such as the Muslim

Brotherhood, ideologically reject the very idea of integration in Western societies. Some specific ethnic and cultural groups, like the Somalis, are simply difficult to integrate in foreign societies. Pakistanis in the United Kingdom remain very close to developments in their home country, as do Turks. With Pakistan becoming increasingly radicalized, Pakistanis in Europe are affected. In contrast, Turks in Europe, coming from a largely secular society at home, are less likely to be influenced by fellow Muslims from other cultures—and indeed remain loyal to the influence of secularist Ankara.

The level of popular and social acceptance of Muslims in Europe in general—and in some countries in particular—has diminished over the past decade, just as the number of Muslim residents has grown. There are many reasons for this, just as there are a number of manifestations.

The reasons include, first of all, the widespread public perception—in countries as diverse as the United Kingdom, France, Spain, and the Netherlands—that the Muslim community harbors significant numbers of Islamist radicals, including terrorists, and does not react strongly enough against their presence. In certain cases, Europeans have been startled by the vehement reaction of Muslim communities to specific events. England, for example, witnessed mass demonstrations demanding the death of author Salman Rushdie, who was accused of insulting Islam in his novel *The Satanic Verses*. In Denmark, and across Europe, even larger demonstrations— some of them violent—occurred after a Danish newspaper published cartoons deemed insulting to the prophet Muhammad and to Islam. Members of the newspaper's staff as well as the cartoonists were threatened with death. Native Europeans see such demonstrations as hostile to their tradition of freedom of speech.

British writer Salman Rushdie. The publication of Rushdie's 1988 novel *The Satanic Verses* sparked angry demonstrations among some European Muslims, who said the book was blasphemous. When Iran's religious leader, the Ayatollah Ruhollah Khomeini, called for Rushdie's death, the author was forced to go into hiding.

Europeans also found it troubling to discover that Muslim residents or citizens (many born in Britain, France, or elsewhere on the continent) were personally involved in fighting (and committing atrocities) in Chechnya, Bosnia, Kashmir, or India; in planning terrorist attacks against the United States; or in being trained by the thousands at al-Qaeda camps in Afghanistan and later in Pakistan.

Finally, and most importantly, the terrorist attacks in Madrid (March 2004) and London (July 2005), which were conducted by Muslims born in those countries or legal immigrants, raised serious questions about the loyalty of a segment of the Muslim population in Europe. And when Europe-based Muslims were involved in suicide bombings in Israel, India, the United States, and Pakistan, and imams living in England engaged in open recruiting for al-Qaeda, public hostility could not but grow.

The reaction took various forms. In some countries, such as Denmark, Austria, and the Netherlands, anti-immigrant parties saw their voting power grow spectacularly. As a result, Muslim immigration was curtailed (in Denmark), surveillance of Muslim communities increased (everywhere), imams were expelled or controlled (France, the Netherlands, Germany), and the very idea of multiculturalism—the view that all cultures are equally worthy of respect—came under attack everywhere. The fact that in most countries the established or recognized Muslim organizations chose to complain about crackdowns on radicals rather than condemning them did not help either. It should be pointed out that, contrary to some media opinions, Europe is not turning racist (let alone that Islam is not a racial category) and the actual racists, like the British National Party (BNP), remain a fringe element everywhere. "Our society changes, and that is good," a member of France's Parliament noted.

Be it that [France] gets richer from the contributions of those who wish to live with us and whom we freely accept! But it must not be forgotten that living with us also means living like us. The first duty of immigrants is to respect the culture of the country that has received them. And this is not negotiable. . . . We are, we remain "Gauls." Thus, it must be possible to affirm that to freely practice one's religion in places of worship does not mean the power to build new minarets, flags of a conquering Islam and a Sharia [Islamic law] opposed to the laws of the Republic.

The Future of
Muslims in Europe

The approach of European governments to the issue of Muslim communities' integration varies widely. The British, for instance, pursue a multiculturalist policy. It allows, and even encourages, Muslim communities to pursue their own customs and practices, including special treatment of Muslim students in schools (special meals, free time for Ramadan prayers, and so on). Some prominent Britons—like Rowan Williams, the Archbishop of Canterbury—even suggest that elements of Sharia should be accepted in Britain. By contrast, the French, for whom complete separation of church and state is a constitutional principle, have banned all religious symbols in public schools, including the Muslim scarf, especially since it is also perceived as a symbol of women's oppression. The other European states are somewhere between British multiculturalism and French assimilationism, with most leaning the French

In France, Muslim students in public schools are forbidden to wear the *hijab*, the traditional Islamic head covering for women.

way during the past few years. On the other hand, more than half of all Muslims in France see themselves as French first and Muslim second. By comparison, 80 percent of Muslims in Britain consider themselves Muslim first.

Curbing the Integration of Muslims in Europe

In March 2006 the Netherlands introduced new requirements for would-be immigrants. These included a large fee ($420) and a compulsory viewing of a video on life in the country, which contained scenes of gays kissing and nude women. "This isn't education, it's provocation," complained Abdu Menebhi, chairman of Emcemo, a Moroccan interest group in Amsterdam. "The new law has one goal: to stop the flow of immigrants, especially by Muslims from countries like Morocco and Turkey." In so stating, he confirmed the very fears that led the government to introduce the test—that Moroccans and Turks automatically feel "provoked" by what ordinary Dutchmen consider part of daily life.

In Germany, at about the same time, the state of Hessen introduced a test about German culture for would-be immigrants. Questions asked the prospective immigrants to, for example, identify three German philosophers, a poem by Goethe, a German Nobel Prize winner, and the doctor who discovered the cholera virus. Volker Bouffier, the state's interior minister, explained, "Anyone who wants to acquire German citizenship should have gone through an extensive consideration of our country and our system of values and have accepted them. The government has to make certain that applicants want to be German citizens—and not just outsiders who live at home in a parallel society."

This opinion was echoed by Chancellor Angela Merkel, who said, "The state can ask whether citizenship choice is a conscious choice or not." However, since national immigration rules could only be decided by consensus among Germany's states, it is unlikely that the rules proposed by Hessen (and Baden-Württemberg) would be accepted, considering the opposition from Social Democratic leaders, both at the national level and in places they govern, like Schleswig-Holstein.

The complex nature of Muslim organizations in Europe is underscored by Milli Gorus, considered by many the largest radical Islamic religious association on the continent. Both Turkey and Germany consider it extremist, but it does control some 300

A view of Amsterdam's red light district. European societies' more liberal attitudes toward gender relations and sexuality (including legalized prostitution in countries such as the Netherlands and Germany) offend some Muslims living in Europe.

mosques and prayer rooms in Germany alone and more in the Netherlands and Belgium, and its leader is a former prime minister of Turkey. It is openly opposed to the integration of Turks in Germany but remains legal.

On the other hand, Muslims in Europe, insofar as they choose to participate in politics, are far from powerless. As of 2008, the leader of the Greens, one of Germany's important parties, was of Turkish origin. In addition, the deputy mayor of Amsterdam and two Dutch ministers, European Parliament members from Germany and France, and the French minister of Justice, were all Muslims.

Turkey, which is geographically and historically partly European and partly Asian, has for decades applied to join the European Union. And for decades its application has been delayed, conditioned, and postponed. Because Turks, or Turkish citizens (since many Turkish citizens in Germany or the Netherlands are in fact Kurds hostile to Turkey, one has to make a sharp distinction), are massively represented among Muslims in Europe, especially in Germany and the Netherlands, the issue of accepting so many millions of EU citizens free to travel and settle in Europe has become political, cultural, and indeed social. Not surprisingly, the countries with the largest Turkish communities (Germany, the Netherlands, and France) object most strongly to Ankara's membership, while Britain and others, interested in strategic issues rather than affected by Turkish immigrant social challenges, support it.

Terrorism as an Obstacle to Integration

It is impossible to discuss Muslims in Europe and their status and public perceptions without mentioning the issue of Islamist terrorism. While it is obviously true that most Muslims, in

Europe and elsewhere, are neither terrorists nor supporters of terrorism, it is also true that from the mid-1990s on, most major terrorist attacks in Europe were perpetrated by Muslims claiming to be engaged in a war against the West. For most native Europeans, to be reluctant to engage with Muslims in their own country because of Islamist terrorism is not "racism." Two spectacular cases influenced the public mind, and not only in the countries where they occurred: the Madrid train bombings of March 11, 2004, and the London subway bombings of July 2005. These incidents—together with the September 11, 2001, attacks in the United States—brought the issue of Islamist terror home to many Europeans.

Those attacks made the European public aware of the presence of an extensive Islamist terrorist network in Europe, linked to al-Qaeda and its various North African and Pakistani associates. Moreover, they also brought to the public's attention the presence of an extensive network of radical imams, most of them based in England, engaged in recruiting and fund-raising for terrorist groups. Most of these people—like Abu Qatada, a Palestinian asylum seeker; Abu Bakri, a Lebanese; and Abu Hamza, an Egyptian—used their positions, and the taxpayers' money, to recruit and indoctrinate local Muslims. Following training in Pakistan or Afghanistan, many of these recruits were sent on missions (often suicidal) to places such as Chechnya, Bosnia, Israel, and India. The concentration of such individuals in England (as distinct from the United Kingdom) and the British legal system's inability to deal with them led to the notion of "Londonistan," especially as some British Muslims were also involved in attempted attacks against the United States (for example, Richard Reid, aka Abdul Raheem, who was arrested in December 2001 after trying to blow up an airliner over the Atlantic with his explosive-filled shoe).

Conclusions

Muslims in Europe present special challenges to the receiving societies. On the one hand, their large numbers and distinct cultures and religious practices raise new questions in previously homogeneous European societies lacking experience in receiving large numbers of culturally and socially alien immigrants. On the other hand, those immigrants often have the support, open or not, of foreign states, and exhibit a degree of religious devotion Europe has long lost. It is said, for instance, that in Britain there are more

A march celebrating Milad an-Nabi, the birthday of the Prophet Muhammad, Buckinghamshire, England, March 15, 2009.

Muslims in mosques on Friday that there are Anglicans in church on Sunday. And it is clear that Islam is the fastest-growing religion in Europe—if not the only religion that is growing at all.

Then there are specific radical Muslim claims in Europe, the most significant being that since Islam cannot accept the loss of control over previously Muslim-ruled areas, the Iberian Peninsula (or Al-Andalus) should be returned to its past Muslim rule. Whether that is a serious demand or not, claims by Muslims in Spain that they have a right to pray at the former Grand Mosque in Córdoba (which has been a Catholic cathedral since 1236) only intensify European anxieties.

Demographics are another problem. With declining birthrates among native Europeans—in some countries below replacement levels—and high birthrates among immigrant Muslims, many Europeans are afraid that they may become a minority in their own countries. The fear, more often than not, has been exaggerated and used by populist parties as an argument against immigration.

Chapter Notes

p. 33: "we want to give our support . . ." Ben Sills, "Cathedral May See Return of Muslims," *The Guardian*, April 19, 2004.

p. 33: "The problem of Islamophobia . . ." Abdennur Prado, "La Islamofobia es el Fascismo del Siglo XXI," *Mundoarabe*, January 24, 2005. http://www.argenpress.info/nota.asp?num=017980

p. 33: "an umbrella organization . . ." The Muslim Council of Britain. http://www.mcb.org.uk/

p. 34: "a vibrant coalition . . ." Ibid.

p. 37: "Muslims still only make up . . ." *Pew Forum on Religion & Public Life, An Uncertain Road: Muslims and the Future of Europe, 2005.* http://pewforum.org/docs/index.php?DocID=60

p. 44: "Our society changes . . ." Jérôme Rivière, "Le multiculturalisme des imbéciles: Sommée de renier son histoire, la France apparaît comme une nation en état de coma culturel dépassé," *Le Figaro*, December 30, 2005.

p. 48: "This isn't education . . ." Gregory Crouch, "A Candid Dutch Film May Be Too Scary for Immigrants," *New York Times*, March 16, 2006.

p. 48: "Anyone who wants to acquire . . ." Luke Harding, "Want a German Passport? Then Get Revising, Says State Minister," *The Guardian*, March 16, 2006.

p. 48: "The state can ask . . ." "Merkel Signals Green Light for Controversial Citizenship Test," *Turkish Daily News*, March 20, 2006.

Chronology

1988: Indian-born British author Salman Rushdie publishes *The Satanic Verses*, a novel some Muslims say insults Islam. Muslims in England demonstrate against Rushdie.

1989: Iran's Supreme Leader, the Ayatollah Ruhollah Khomeini, issues a fatwa (a legal opinion or decree from an Islamic leader) calling for devout Muslims to kill Salman Rushdie. Fearing for his life, the author goes into hiding.

1994: On December 24, members of Algeria's Armed Islamic Group (GIA) hijack an Air France jetliner. The four terrorists were killed during a rescue effort.

1995: In August, GIA members bomb a Paris metro station, killing 8 people and injuring more than 80.

1996: On December 3, GIA militants bomb a French subway train, killing 4 people and injuring 86.

2001: In December, Richard Reid, a British Muslim, tries to explode a bomb concealed in his sneakers during an American Airlines flight from Paris to Miami.

2004: In February, a Dutch-born Muslim fanatic murders filmmaker Theo van Gogh in Amsterdam. On March 11, bombs explode on four commuter trains in Madrid, killing more than 200 people and injuring 1,400. Those responsible are Moroccan, Algerian and Tunisian Islamists.

2005: On July 7, British-born Muslims with ties to Pakistan bomb London's transportation system, killing 52 people and injuring approximately 2,000. After the October publication by a Danish newspaper of 12 cartoons depicting the Prophet Muhammad and Islam negatively, Muslims across

Europe protest; some call for the cartoonists and newspaper editors to be killed.

2007: Nyamko Sabuni, a Muslim woman of African origin, is appointed Minister for Integration and Gender Equality of Sweden. In the Netherlands, Turkish-born Nebahat Albayrak is appointed State Secretary for Justice, and Moroccan-born Ahmed Aboutaleb is appointed State Secretary for Social Affairs and Employment. In France, Rachida Dati, a Muslim woman of Moroccan and Algerian descent, is appointed Minister of Justice.

2008: Cem Ozdemir, an ethnic Turk, is elected co-chairman of Germany's Green Party.

Glossary

demographic—relating to the statistical characteristics (such as size, density, and growth) of human populations.

European Union (EU)—an association of states subscribing to the Treaty of Rome (1957, as modified); it includes 27 countries: Belgium, Luxembourg, the Netherlands, France, Italy, Germany, the United Kingdom, Ireland, Austria, Spain, Portugal, Greece, Slovenia, Slovakia, the Czech Republic, Hungary, Bulgaria, Romania, Latvia, Estonia, Lithuania, Denmark, Finland, Sweden, Malta, Cyprus, and Poland. The EU's executive headquarters are in Brussels, Belgium; its Parliament and courts are in Strasbourg, France.

Islamophobia—fear or hatred of Islam.

multiculturalism—the belief that a variety of cultures can coexist peacefully within a single society; advocacy or promotion of cultural pluralism rather than a single national culture.

Salafi—a Muslim who considers Islam as practiced in its early decades (specifically, during the time of the first three generations of Muslims) to be the pure form of the religion. Salafists reject as invalid any beliefs or practices in Islam that developed after the seventh century.

secularism—the belief that religion, religious organizations, and religious leaders should have no role in the political and civic affairs of a country.

Shia—the smaller of Islam's main branches, which broke from the larger Sunni branch during the seventh century over the issue of who should succeed the Prophet Muhammad as Islam's political and spiritual leader. Today about 14 percent of Muslims worldwide follow Shia Islam, though Shiites constitute the majority in the countries of Iran, Iraq, and Bahrain.

Sunni—a Muslim belonging to Islam's larger, orthodox branch. An estimated 85 percent of Muslims worldwide are Sunnis.

Further Reading

Al Sayyid, Nezar, and Manuel Castells, editors. *Muslim Europe or Euro-Islam: Politics, Culture, and Citizenship in the Age of Globalization.* Lanham, Md.: Lexington Books, 2002.

Buruma, Ian. *Murder in Amsterdam: The Death of Theo van Gogh and the Limits of Tolerance.* New York: Penguin Books, 2006.

Hirsi Ali, Ayaan. *The Caged Virgin: An Emancipation Proclamation of Women and Islam.* New York/London: Free Press, 2006.

Husain, Ed. *The Islamist.* London: Penguin Books, 2007.

Kepel, Gilles. *The War for Muslim Minds: Islam and the West.* Cambridge, Mass.: The Belknap Press of Harvard University Press, 2004.

Radu, Michael. *Europe's Ghost: Tolerance, Jihadism, and the West.* New York: Encounter Books, 2009.

Internet Resources

http://meria.idc.ac.il/

An online magazine that covers a wide variety topics in international affairs, including Islam in Europe.

http://www.fpri.org/

The website of the Foreign Policy Research Institute, with lots of essays on radical Islam and terrorism, plus a database of think tanks.

http://www.isn.ethz.ch/

The website of the Center for Security Studies, a think tank based in Zurich, Switzerland, with links to essays from think tanks around the world.

Publisher's Note: The Web sites listed on this page were active at the time of publication. The publisher is not responsible for Web sites that have changed their address or discontinued operation since the date of publication. The publisher reviews and updates the Web sites each time the book is reprinted.

Index

Numbers in **bold italics** refer to captions.